*Quick*GUIDES
everything you need to know...fast

Meetings

by Jan Hatch

reviewed by Jinny Gender

WIREMILL
PUBLISHING LTD

Across the world the organizations and institutions that fundraise to finance their work are referred to in many different ways. They are charities, non-profits or not-for-profit organizations, non-governmental organizations (NGOs), voluntary organizations, academic institutions, agencies, etc. For ease of reading, we have used the term Nonprofit Organization, Organization or NPO as an umbrella term throughout the *Quick* Guide series. We have also used the spellings and punctuation used by the author.

Published by
Wiremill Publishing Ltd.
Edenbridge, Kent TN8 5PS, UK
info@wiremillpublishing.com
www.wircmillpublishing.com
www.quickguidesonline.com

British Library Cataloguing in Publication Data
A catalogue record for this book is available from the British Library.

ISBN Number 1-905053-37-1

Printed by Rhythm Consolidated Berhad, Malaysia
Cover Design by Jennie de Lima and Edward Way
Design by Colin Woodman

Disclaimer of Liability
The author, reviewer and publisher shall have neither liability nor responsibility to any person or entity with respect to any loss or damage caused or alleged to be caused directly or indirectly by the information contained in this book. While the book is as accurate as possible, there may be errors, omissions or inaccuracies.

Contents

INTRODUCTION

Meetings are a way of life in nonprofit organizations (NPOs). Even in the smallest organization, there will be a wide range of meetings taking place on a regular basis: planning meetings, staff meetings, members' meetings, board meetings, committee meetings, annual general meetings, meetings with funding bodies and supporters, and meetings with government officials. There may be even more meetings in nonprofit organizations than in most businesses because of the number of people who need to be involved in the various activities of the organization.

However, many people working in NPOs would agree that there seems to be an endless series of meetings, and most of them are a complete waste of time. A common complaint: "When will I ever get to spend time on my *real* job?" Those who have studied meetings report that up to 53 percent of the time spent in meetings is unproductive.

So why don't we just give up on meetings? The short answer is, we can't. Every NPO needs a group of committed and dedicated people who are willing to work together to achieve the goals and aspirations of the organization. All of these people, whether paid or voluntary, need to meet one another on a regular basis to make plans and decisions, to govern, to be accountable, to review and to evaluate.

We can't do without meetings but we can make them more successful. To do that, we need to make them more than just a gathering of people; we need to make them effective and useful. This *Quick*Guide will give the tools you need to improve any meeting, whether it involves 2, 20 or 200 people.

There are many reasons for holding meetings:

- To decide on policy and strategy.
- To agree on objectives, priorities and plans.
- To inform and report on activities and external developments.
- To monitor and evaluate progress.
- To discuss problems and come up with solutions.
- To share views and opinions.
- To provide support and advice.
- To get feedback or to evaluate performance.
- To discuss and agree on professional development.

Most meetings will include a mixture of the above, depending on the purposes and desired outcomes and those attending the meetings.

Many times the reasons for holding meetings become lost. This is particularly true for groups that meet on a regular basis with the same people attending each time. The agenda for this kind of meeting will frequently have fixed items that are dealt with at every meeting.

One-on-one or small-group meetings are often impromptu and happen with little or insufficient consideration of the reason for the meeting. Taking a moment to think about why the meeting is being held, even if it's done at the beginning of a meeting rather than in advance, is valuable in order to make the meeting more successful and productive for those attending.

If possible, no meeting should be held without a clear idea of the reason why. Those invited to attend should ensure they know the reason or reasons before their attendance. This will not only make the meeting go more smoothly but will also help make sure the appropriate people are actually attending it.

The five key elements of a successful meeting are:

- Well-defined purposes and outcomes
- Good preparation
- Appropriate paperwork (pre- and post-meeting)
- Leadership
- Discipline

1. **Defining purpose and outcome** is the first and most important step of all. With a clearly stated and understood purpose for the meeting and with the intended outcome from the meeting clearly defined, all those attending a meeting will be able to contribute and participate with confidence and to the best of their ability.

2. **Preparation** involves getting the right people to the meeting and making sure they know what they are there to do. Having a clear purpose (see No. 1 above) will enable you to decide who should attend and what kind of information they need to bring to the meeting in order to participate fully in the discussion and decision making.

3. **Paperwork** includes the invitation to or notification of the meeting, travel and accommodation instructions, the agenda and any relevant supporting documents and/or reports, financial statements, and background materials related to the agenda items, all of which will be needed to inform the participants. It also includes the minutes of the previous meeting and a written record of action points or plans arising from that meeting. Paperwork can be distributed in hard copy by mail, by email or fax, or can be hand-delivered depending on the requirements of the organization. No matter how it is distributed, it should be complete and sent far enough in advance to give participants time to put the meeting in their schedule, plan their participation and make travel plans if necessary.

4. **Leadership** is the second-most important element in any successful meeting. A good leader or chair keeps the meeting focused on its purposes and outcomes. The

leader maintains a position of objectivity and manages any conflict in a professional manner. He or she makes sure that all the participants contribute and that no one person or viewpoint dominates. He or she makes sure that everyone is clear about the decisions made. Finally, the leader will make sure that the meeting begins and ends on time.

5. ***Discipline*** is required of all those attending a meeting. This means being prepared, understanding the purposes and outcomes of the meeting and the ground rules for participating, and reading the agenda and the supporting papers. The main role of all those attending any meeting is to respect the chair and work with him or her to achieve the purposes and outcomes of the meeting, even if they personally disagree or have an alternative view to express.

The following is not an exhaustive list of the meetings you may attend but highlights some of the most common. Obviously many of the meetings you participate in will be unique to your organization or workplace. Remember, the five elements outlined previously apply to all meetings.

The purposes and outcomes of some meetings are defined by the particular legal frameworks within which the NPO exists. These will vary from one country to another; sometimes, even in the same country, there will be different rules for different kinds of NPOs.

The most formal meeting held by an organization is generally the annual meeting or annual general meeting. It may be a legal requirement in your country that your organization holds one each year. Who attends, what is on the agenda, and how decisions are made and then recorded are often defined within a strict set of rules and regulations. There may also be rules about how motions and resolutions for actions should be put forward, how debate should be conducted, how conflicts or differences of opinion should be resolved, and how decisions should be recorded and implemented. When preparing for a meeting of this kind, all the relevant rules and regulations should be taken into account.

A second type of required meeting may be set forth in an NPO's constitution or a written set of formal rules. These define the purpose and frequency of meetings for groups established by those rules; these groups include governing councils, boards or management committees, advisory boards or committees, and subcommittees. In addition, these documents will frequently define the membership of these bodies as well as the roles and responsibilities of the officers and members of these groups.

Reviewer's Comment
In some countries, the formal rules under which an organization operates are called bylaws. In other countries, they may be known under other names. In some countries, there are external rules (one such set is called Robert's Rules of Order) that are neither statutory nor the rules of the organization but under which meetings are held. In some cases, these rules are so widespread that the chair and board members familiarize themselves with them

before sitting on boards. Large organizations have been known to hire an expert to sit in on meetings, particularly the annual meeting, to make sure that everything is exactly as it should be procedurally. Ensure you know whether there are rules in the country under which your organization operates.

In general, committees will meet on a regular basis with defined responsibilities for reviewing the work of the organization, setting plans and budgets, monitoring progress, and dealing with matters of policy.

Staff meetings take many forms and have a variety of purposes but generally are used to share information and news, report on activities and upcoming events, provide updates on progress, and promote shared approaches to the vision and mission of the organization.

Team meetings allow smaller groups of people to focus on particular objectives or goals, to monitor progress, and to report on activities and tasks.

One-on-one meetings are often used by managers to keep track of the activities of individual members of staff, to provide opportunities for professional development and to discuss performance-related issues.

Most NPOs will also hold a wide range of meetings with *volunteers, members, stakeholders* and *service users*. There are many purposes for these meetings depending on the organizations, but they may include the following:

- Reporting on activities and initiatives

- Promoting understanding of and commitment to the organization

- Discussing matters of concern

- Celebrating successes

- Reporting on changes in the external environment and discussing the potential impact of such changes

- Getting feedback on programs and projects

- Skills training

- Consulting on planned activities or new developments

STEPS FOR HOLDING MEETINGS

Step 1 – Defining Purposes and Outcomes

Meetings with clear purposes and outcomes are rarely a waste of time. If the meeting is a regular one but with no external requirements, the purposes and outcomes should be reviewed on a regular basis in the event that:

- The entire meeting has become irrelevant and can be discontinued.

- Certain purposes and outcomes have become irrelevant.

- Certain purposes and outcomes have changed.

Regular reviews of the purposes and outcomes of such meetings are vital to keep them relevant and interesting. It is also essential that new participants understand the purposes and outcomes for the meeting, even though these may be obvious to long-term members.

If the meeting is not a regular one, then those calling for it need to evaluate, sometimes with the help of those planning to attend, the purposes and outcomes expected. If anyone attending a meeting feels it is a waste of his or her time, then this will have an impact on the value of the meeting.

Step 2 – Preparation

The best way to prepare for any meeting is to start with a simple checklist. Depending on the meeting and the organization, the checklist might contain the following questions:

- What is the purpose of the meeting and the desired outcome?

- What are the limitations within which this meeting takes place?

- Who should attend the meeting?

- When should the meeting take place (date and time)?

- What is the appropriate venue?

- Will refreshments be needed?

- What paperwork needs to be provided?

- Do any of those attending have special needs?

- Is the venue properly accessible to everyone?

- Is any equipment needed, e.g., projectors, screens, audio equipment?

Who Should Attend

Some groups, such as boards of trustees or management committees, will have a defined membership of people who are required to attend meetings. In addition, it may be desirable or necessary to invite additional people with specialized knowledge or expertise to contribute to particular agenda items.

In general, it is a good idea to avoid a routine list of people who are always invited to meetings of particular groups. A regular review of the membership of more informal groups is necessary to make sure that those who attend meetings have something specific to contribute.

Time and Place

Once you have confirmed who is attending the meeting, you must work out a suitable time and place for the meeting. For groups that meet regularly, it is generally advisable to agree on specific dates and times on an annual basis. You will need to find a venue that is easily accessible, is big enough to accommodate everyone, and has the necessary equipment and facilities.

Make sure the room is booked and, if necessary, refreshments and/or meals are organized. The room should be big enough for everyone to sit comfortably, it should be quiet and, if possible, have some natural light. Be clear about what equipment you need and check that it is in good working order before the meeting. Make sure the lighting is adequate and that people can see properly from wherever they are sitting. There should be enough elbowroom for everyone and space for their documents and writing materials. Water should be available. Depending on the length of the meeting, regular breaks should be scheduled.

Making sure that those who attend the meeting feel welcome is very important. Greet people as they arrive, particularly if the venue is new to them. If this is not possible, ensure that there are signs posted and/or that reception personnel are informed about the meeting and have a list of those who are attending. If it is a new group that is meeting for the first time, you might consider having name tags and/or cards for each person.

People work better in an atmosphere that is professional and cordial. With good preparation, everyone can get down to the business of the meeting quickly and in comfort.

Continued on Page 12

Reviewer's Comment

Do note special requirements of participants such as food and access. Some countries have specific laws regarding disability or access to meetings with which you must comply.

Step 3 – Paperwork

Invitation/Notification of the Meeting

You should make sure that an invitation or notification of the meeting is sent to all participants in good time – not so far in advance that the details are forgotten and not so late that people are unavailable to attend the meeting. Include information about the venue and contact details, along with details of when the meeting is scheduled to start and finish and the timing of breaks.

Reviewer's Comment

Notice of the time and place of some meetings must be publicly advertised and open to the public. Some meetings may be videotaped and available at a later date. Also, the planners must consider other local laws and customs.

Instructions for Travel and Accommodations

If the venue is a new or unfamiliar one or is in a location that involves travel, then send detailed travel instructions including maps to all participants. You may also wish to include information about parking and/or public transportation.

If overnight accommodations are required, make sure participants know who will be making those arrangements. It is important to make sure that any special needs are taken into account.

Agenda

There are several reasons why it makes good sense to spend some time thinking about the agenda for all meetings, even informal ones. The main purpose of the agenda is to organize the business of the meeting so that everyone who attends will know what items are going to be dealt with before they get there. Careful preparation of the agenda gives the chair a chance to set priorities and ensure there is enough time available to deal thoroughly with all of the most important matters.

In many cases, the agenda will have standard items that are common to every meeting. These may be prescribed by the rules of the organization. These items will form the basis for the agenda and will probably include the following:

- Chair's introduction and welcome
- Apologies for absence from the meeting
- Minutes of the last meeting
- Matters arising from the minutes
- Correspondence
- Reports
- Additional items for discussion and/or decision
- Any other business
- Date of the next meeting

Refer to the minutes of the previous meeting when drafting the agenda so that any matters that need continuing discussion or further decision can be included. Giving each item a title and a number helps to keep items in order, and any reports or discussion papers can be numbered to correspond with the associated agenda item number.

Another way of keeping the meeting focused is to describe each individual agenda item in terms of what the intended outcome is:

- For information only
- For discussion or canvassing views
- For problem solving
- To make a decision on the action to be taken
- To report back on actions taken since the last meeting
- To ratify decisions made by a subcommittee or by management
- To review objectives or actions

Send the agenda out to all participants before the meeting so that anyone who cannot attend is able to send in comments. If anyone wants an item to be considered for the agenda, make sure they contact the chair or the person organizing the agenda in advance of the meeting.

Reviewer's Comment
Depending on local law and/or the bylaws of the organization, some agendas cannot be changed.

Continued on Page 14

REPORTS AND DISCUSSION PAPERS

Most formal meetings deal with routine items that involve the preparation and review of reports. Agenda items will often include the following reports:

- Treasurer's or financial

- Management or manager's

- Subcommittee or advisory group

- Progress on individual, team or departmental objectives or plans

- Project or program reports

- Discussion papers on issues requiring decisions

The *treasurer's or financial report* usually consists of a set of financial accounts which should be easy to read and in a format that is the same from one meeting to the next. These reports should highlight any major differences between the budgeted amounts and the actual amounts of either income or expenditures, and they should provide an explanation for those differences. They should include a balance sheet, information about reserves or surplus funds, and any information about funding applications that are due or problems with the flow of cash into the organization. In different countries, there may be specific requirements for financial reports.

Management reports should be in a standard format so that those preparing them provide consistent and useful information to the meeting participants. The report needs to highlight any major issues, concerns or events.

Subcommittee or advisory group reports might take the form of formal reports from the groups involved or minutes from their own meetings, with recommendations or items for approval highlighted.

Papers should include reports and recommendations for decisions by the group in a clear format. The format could include the following headings:

- Title and author of the paper

- Date (of the meeting at which the paper is to be considered)

- Lead responsibility for implementation

- Desired result (for information or decision)

- Executive summary

- Recommendation(s)

- Discussion and/or background of the activity

- Resource implications: financial and other

- Risk implications

- Impact on other policies, projects or programs

- Process and timetable for implementation

- Expected outcomes and/or key performance indicators for judging success

- Monitoring and review arrangements

Ideally, no report should be longer than four sides of paper and should be presented to the meeting by the person who wrote it.

MINUTES OR NOTES – RECORDING ACTION POINTS AND DECISIONS

The minutes or notes are the permanent written record of the decisions that were made and the business that was conducted at the meeting.

If there is a secretary, it is his or her job to take the minutes and prepare them for distribution. If there isn't a designated secretary, then one of those attending the meeting will need to take on this job.

Unless it is a very formal and legally regulated meeting, the minutes should be simple and written in plain language. They should be brief, accurate and objective. *They should not be a verbatim account of the discussions that took place or what everyone said at the meeting.*

The key things that should be recorded in the minutes are:

- Nature and type of meeting

- Day, date and time

- Place

- Names of those present

- Apologies for absence from the meeting

- Reports received

- Decisions made and/or resolutions passed

- Actions agreed on and who will be responsible for implementing them

Continued on Page 16

■ Summary of the key points of the discussions, including any dissenting opinions or points

■ Time the meeting ended

■ Date and time of the next meeting

Do not insert or include anything in the minutes that occurred or developed after or outside the meeting.

Produce the minutes as soon as possible after the meeting. It is important that the chair review a draft of the minutes to ensure their accuracy, particularly to ensure that decisions and action points have been properly recorded. It is not advisable to circulate a draft to everyone who attended the meeting for comments unless this is the chair's wish. Once the minutes have been agreed on, distribute them to all the participants as soon as possible.

Reviewer's Comment
Looking at previous minutes is useful because this will help provide continuity for regular meetings.

CHAIRING A MEETING

Every meeting needs to have a leader or chair. Though it may be tempting to do without a chair, especially for smaller meetings, don't. It is vital that someone takes responsibility for the agenda, for keeping the discussion on each item focused, for making sure the ground rules for the meeting are followed and, most importantly, for making sure the meeting's purposes and objectives are met.

The chair of the board or management committee of an NPO has a specific role defined by the organization's constitution and the relevant legal requirements. This role will include a wide variety of responsibilities, including chairing meetings of the board and other committees. The chair's skill and experience in chairing meetings will have an impact on the organization as a whole by demonstrating that he or she is capable and able; this confidence will carry over into other activities.

APPOINTING OR CHOOSING A CHAIR

There are likely to be rules about how someone is appointed or elected to the position of chairperson of an NPO board or management committee. These will usually be found in the constitution or governing document.

This document may also specify the mechanism for filling the role of chair for other committees, groups or teams.

Senior management team meetings and department or division meetings are common to most organizations, and they are often chaired by the CEO, manager or department head. Project or task-group meetings, professional group meetings and case conferences, for example, may not have an obvious chair. Depending on the type of group, a chair may emerge from one of the following:

■ The longest-serving participant

■ The highest-ranking participant

■ The person most familiar with chairing meetings

■ The person calling the meeting

Even an ad hoc meeting should be led by someone. Rotating the chair is often done to give individuals the experience of chairing a meeting. If this is the aim, then you should make sure that proper guidance and support are provided to ensure that the person knows what is expected of him or her and understands the basic skills needed to fulfill the responsibilities.

Continued on Page 18

CHAIRING A MEETING

PREPARING TO CHAIR THE MEETING

No matter what kind of meeting, it is vitally important that the chair spends time preparing for it. In particular, it is essential that the chair be involved in planning the agenda because this is the tool he or she will use to give the meeting direction and shape.

The chair should know in advance who will be attending the meeting, what organization they come from and/or what position they hold, and what, if any, special expertise or knowledge they have to contribute. Ideally the chair should know in advance if someone is not able to attend the meeting for some reason. Finally the chair should know whether any special presentations are scheduled, when breaks are planned, and what time the meeting is scheduled to begin and end.

Whether it is a regular or a one-off meeting, the chair should spend a bit of time making notes on each agenda item before the meeting. These may include:

- Summary of the background to the item
- The key issue to be dealt with
- The objective of the item

- Strong points
- Weak points
- Key questions
- Options
- The desired outcome

RULES GOVERNING THE MEETING

It is important for everyone attending the meeting to be clear about the rules under which the meeting will be conducted. The chair is responsible for making sure that these are agreed on and followed. Rules may include the following:

- Meetings begin and end on time.
- No mobile phones or pocket or personal computers are allowed.
- At all times, show respect for each participant and his or her contribution.
- No derogatory or discriminatory comments may be made.
- One person speaks at a time; don't interrupt.
- Keep contributions brief and to the point; do not repeat what others have said.
- Everyone gets to speak on an item before general discussion begins.

Chairing a Meeting

- Be aware of and declare any potential or actual conflicts of interest before discussion of an agenda item begins.

- Questions are encouraged.

Running the Meeting

At all times, the chair must maintain the focus of the meeting. Sticking to business is the only way the purposes and outcomes will be achieved. This also keeps the meeting moving along and gives the chair the chance to cut off anyone who rambles, disrupts, distracts or strays from the point.

There are seven key points to remember.

1. Do not get bogged down.

In most meetings, the first item on the agenda after the apologies for absence from the meeting is the approval of the minutes.

Once the minutes are approved, the chair signs them on behalf of the group, and they are filed in a minute book for future reference.

"Matters arising" is usually the next item on the agenda. This item should only consist of feedback on any decisions or actions that were approved. This item should not be used as an opportunity to reopen a discussion or to review the decisions that were taken at the previous meeting.

In general, routine matters should be dealt with early in the meeting. It is the chair's job to make sure that these items are dealt with quickly and efficiently so that there is ample time to spend on the more important items on the agenda.

2. Beware of "Any Other Business."

This agenda item can provide an opening for people to slip in matters of importance at a time when people are getting ready to leave or have already left the meeting. The most effective way of preventing this is to place this item on the agenda near the beginning of the meeting. Another method is to establish a rule that anyone who wants to raise issues for discussion under this item must notify the chair in advance.

3. Emphasize the purpose and define limits.

The chair's manner sets the tone for the whole group, so be businesslike and pleasant but also firm about timing, and be focused on the agenda.

Begin the meeting promptly and professionally. Remember to make any

Continued on Page 20

introductions that need to be made. Don't assume everyone knows one another.

The chair must remain alert at all times. If matters arise in discussions that are important and urgent, then it is vital that they are dealt with in a way that does not disrupt or derail the entire meeting.

If it is a meeting of the board of an NPO, then the chair must always be vigilant about ensuring that the meeting doesn't stray into areas that are the responsibility of management. It can often be difficult for board members to remain clear about their roles, particularly in times of trouble. However, it is vital that board members remain focused on governance and be clear about the scope of their authority.

Reviewer's Comment

Begin on time! Start the meeting exactly on time, even if everyone isn't there. If you don't, you reward the tardy members, which increases that kind of behavior. The chair should be scrupulous about this.

---

4. LISTEN POSITIVELY.

Establishing respectful relationships among those attending is a key role of the chair. Make it clear that everyone has something to contribute and that everyone's views are important. Ensure that any presentations are kept to time and that it is clear when questions can be taken. Encourage participants to ask questions for clarification only, and make it clear that argument and debate are not acceptable at this stage, unless that is the stated purpose of the presentation.

Listen carefully and positively to everyone, writing down any key points or facts that may be relevant to the discussion. These will be needed later for interim and final summaries.

It is the chair's job to keep the discussion on track and to ensure that everyone who has a contribution to make can make it no matter how shy or unconfident they might be. When the chair doesn't listen positively or encourage others to do the same, the opportunity to benefit from the knowledge and experience of all of those involved in the meeting is lost. People who are not listened to will feel that they have wasted their time and that their input is not valued. This has a knock-on, or indirect, effect on their morale and motivation, and on future collaboration and teamwork.

5. PROVIDE INTERIM SUMMARIES.

Interim summaries are one of the most important tools a chair can use as a way of keeping the discussion focused and moving toward the desired outcome. Summaries are a way of making sure that the person taking the minutes is clear about the key points to be documented as the discussion moves on.

Interim summaries are used to:

- Cover a gap in the discussion.
- Simplify something that is complicated or obscure.
- Separate the relevant from the irrelevant.
- Interrupt distracting or disruptive contributions.
- Gain control of the discussion.
- Indicate progress.
- Identify important issues that have not been agreed on or approved so that they can be discussed.
- Confirm agreement or approval.

6. CONFIRM THE DECISIONS AND ACTION POINTS.

A good chair will have some idea, before the meeting even begins, of what decisions or actions need to be agreed on. During the meeting, make sure that all participants understand the issue under discussion and are clear about the decisions to be made. Then confirm that the person taking the minutes makes a note of these key points before moving on to the next item on the agenda.

7. DEAL WITH SHY OR DIFFICULT PEOPLE.

The chair needs to take responsibility for ensuring that all those attending the meeting are encouraged and able to participate to the best of their ability.

It is the chair's job to make sure that everyone is given the space and attention to participate. This is especially important in meetings that include people with disabilities and/or those whose first language is not the language being spoken at the meeting.

Manage carefully but firmly any difficult or argumentative people. It may take several meetings before they get the message that interrupting or banging on the table is not acceptable. Sometimes just listening positively will bring their behavior to a halt. Sometimes having a word with them before the meeting will help defuse any anger or frustration they may feel.

ATTENDING A MEETING

It isn't just the chair's job to make the meeting go well. Participants also have responsibilities. They should:

- Be prepared – read the material and be familiar with the agenda before the meeting.
- Be clear about the purposes and desired outcomes of the meeting.
- Clarify any confusion or questions before the meeting.
- Be clear about their objectives for the meeting.
- Be punctual.
- Follow the ground rules.
- Respect the chair and his or her authority.
- Tactfully ask clarifying questions or present interim summaries if the chair is weak or inexperienced.
- Not just sit there – actively participate.
- Listen carefully.
- Try to time interventions and contributions to make sure they are heard.

Remember every participant has a responsibility for making sure that the objectives of the meeting are met.

Whatever kind of meeting, whether it is a large formal one or a one-on-one session with a colleague, always, always spend some time preparing.

Those making a presentation or speaking on a particular topic should be adequately prepared. Know the purpose of the presentation and keep it short and simple. Keep visual aids simple, too. Make sure to check the equipment to make sure that it works.

Reviewer's Comment
Please do not read visual aids aloud! The speaker should expand and elucidate – the audience can read!

Making presentations is a skill, and anyone needing to do them should both obtain training and practice doing them as often as possible.

CONCLUSION

Meetings can be productive and thought-provoking. They don't have to be a waste of time and energy. With preparation and commitment, energy and enthusiasm, every meeting can be productive. When you next attend a meeting, take note of whether the five steps are being followed. Observe what happens when the meeting's purpose isn't clear or when there hasn't been enough preparation. Notice how difficult it is to make a decision when a report is discussed at the meeting without prior notice or when the chair doesn't keep the discussion focused. Try to actively participate in making a bad meeting more effective.

Developing the ability to run a good meeting is a certain way to improve relationships with colleagues and increase influence at work. It is well worth the time and effort to put the guidance in this *Quick*Guide into practice

... even if only to make the meetings you attend good ones.

JAN HATCH

Jan Hatch has worked in the nonprofit sector for more than 25 years in the US, Canada, the UK and Australia. She has worked in both paid and unpaid positions, mainly in the health, disability and community care sector.

Her first role in the sector was as a member of the board of directors of Nellies Emergency Shelter for Women in Toronto. She went on to be a founding member of the board and the first member of staff of the Women's Legal Education and Action Fund. Moving to the UK in 1986, Jan worked in women's health before setting up and running the first national telephone helpline for carers. In 1992 she went to work at the Multiple Sclerosis Society of Great Britain and Northern Ireland where she was Director of Services for more than seven years. She was instrumental in the development of the *Standards of Healthcare for People with MS*, a publication that has been highly influential in improving health and social services throughout the UK.

Jan was a founding member of the Long Term Medical Conditions Alliance, a trustee of both the Disability Alliance and the Neurological Alliance, and a member of the Services Committee of the Multiple Sclerosis International Federation. Since moving to Sydney, Australia in 2001, she has worked with a number of nonprofit organizations including NCOSS, The Smith Family, Jewishcare and The Fred Hollows Foundation.

Jinny Gender, Reviewer

Jinny Gender has a degree in sociology from Lindenwood College in St. Charles, Missouri, USA. In a nonprofit career spanning 30 years, Jinny has served on dozens of nonprofit boards – as president of many – and worked tirelessly as a volunteer.

In the last 10 years alone, Jinny has served on 20 nonprofit boards including: National Public Radio KWMU in St. Louis, past president; Metro St. Louis Women's Political Caucus, past president; ALIVE, Alternatives to Living in Violent Environments, past president; Lindenwood Alumni Club, past president; Charter board member of the St. Louis County Shelter for Abused Women; Confluence, St. Louis; Magic House, Museum for Children; and Y.E.S., Youth Emergency Service. She has been a hearing tester for the Special School district for 20 years and has had her own weekly talk-radio show on station WGNU in St. Louis for the last 10 years. With a partner, Jinny Gender has her own consulting business, International Charity Consultants.